# Contents

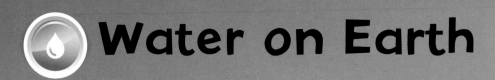 Water on Earth

Most of planet Earth is covered with water.
The oceans hold almost all of this water.
They are very wide and deep.

Boats can sail across the ocean to countries that are very far away.

Plants and animals need water to live. People drink water, and plants take water from the soil.

If there is not a lot of rain, we have to water plants.

◉ Ice

At the north and south of the
Earth, there are huge areas of ice.
This frozen water partly melts in
the summer.

Arctic foxes change colour.
They match the white ice
in winter, and the brown
ground in summer.

A glacier is a huge area of ice and snow. It moves slowly over the land.

Glaciers contain one third of the world's fresh water.

Franz Josef Glacier in New Zealand starts high up in the mountains.

The water cycle

Water from the land and ocean
rises up through the air as vapour.
This water vapour makes clouds.

clouds

soil

ocean

The water falls from the clouds as rain and snow. It flows into the land and ocean, and the water cycle starts again.

rain

river

lake

Rivers

The start of the river is called its source. Most rivers start high in the mountains or hills.

Tiny streams of water join together to form a river.

Rivers get bigger as more streams flow into them. Mud, stones and soil are carried along by the river. This makes the water look less clear.

The Amazon River can be so muddy that people cannot see anything in it.

The Amazon River in South America runs through seven countries.

Waterfalls and lakes

As rivers flow downhill, they sometimes pass over steep rocks. The water falls through the air until it hits the ground again. This falling river is called a waterfall.

The highest waterfall in the world is Angel Falls in Venezuela.

Some rivers run into lakes. Lakes are large areas of water that have land around them. Water often flows out of lakes and continues on to the sea.

Lake Baikal in Russia is the deepest lake in the world.

Animals

Almost half of all types of animal on Earth live in the oceans. The water in the oceans is salty.

Watch out! Some jellyfish have long tentacles that can sting you.

The blue whale is the biggest animal on Earth.

Sea turtles can live for over 200 years.

Many animals live in and around freshwater rivers and lakes. Fresh water is not salty like the ocean.

Piranhas live in rivers in South America. They have very sharp teeth.

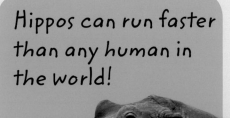

Hippos can run faster than any human in the world!

Drinking water

In most towns and cities, running water comes from lakes and rivers. The water is cleaned before we use it.

You should try to drink 1 litre (four glasses) of water a day.

Drinking fountains give us fresh, clean water.

16

There is clean water deep underground. People dig holes called wells, and bring up this water to drink.

Water pumps make it easier to take water out of wells.

How we use water

We use water at home to wash ourselves, cook food, clean clothes, flush the toilet and for many other things.

You can save water by turning off the tap while you brush your teeth!

Leaving the tap on while brushing your teeth wastes 12 litres of water every day.

Many factories use lots of water to make things such as computers, paper, food and cars. Cold water cools machines, which can get very hot.

Factories can recycle water so that they don't use too much of it.

19

Water pollution

Water pollution happens when people throw rubbish into rivers, lakes and seas. This rubbish can poison the water so it is not safe to drink.

Plastic bottles are the most common cause of water pollution.

Always recycle your bottles! Only 1 in 10 plastic bottles are recycled.

Oil is transported on huge ships.
Sometimes these ships are damaged,
and oil flows into the ocean.
Animals and plants are hurt.

This person is helping to clean oil off a bird.

True or false?

The right answer to all of the true or false questions below can be found in this book. Try to remember what the answers are, and look in the book if you really don't know.

1. Fresh water is salty.
True or **false**?

2. Angel Falls is the highest waterfall in the world.
True or **false**?

3. Clouds are made of water vapour.
True or **false**?

4. The source is the beginning of a river.
True or **false**?

5. Glaciers move very quickly.
True or **false**?

6. Humans and animals can stay alive without water.
True or **false**?

Answers: 1 = false, 2 = true, 3 = true, 4 = true, 5 = false, 6 = false.

Make a rain gauge

You will need:
· a clean, empty large plastic bottle · scissors · sticky tape · water · waterproof pen · ruler

A rain gauge can show how much rain has fallen in a day, a week or a month.

1. Ask an adult to cut the top off the plastic bottle where the slope begins. Turn the top upside down inside the bottle, and stick it in place.

2. Fill the bottom of the bottle with a little bit of water. Mark the point that the water reaches as 0 cm.

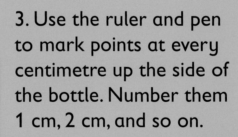

3. Use the ruler and pen to mark points at every centimetre up the side of the bottle. Number them 1 cm, 2 cm, and so on.

4. Leave your rain gauge outside where it can catch the raindrops. Every day, measure how much rain there has been. Record this in a notebook over a week.

Glossary

factory building where things are made by machines

fresh water water that isn't salty

melt change from solid to liquid, such as when ice changes to water

oil a greasy liquid that burns well and is used to power cars

poison substance that can hurt or kill a living thing

recycle send off rubbish to be made into something new, instead of throwing it away

sea an area of salt water at the edge of an ocean, partly surrounded by land

soil top part of the Earth's surface, in which plants grow

stream thin, moving area of water

tentacles long thin body parts that some animals use like arms

waste rubbish or pollution

water vapour when water gets very hot, it turns from a liquid into a gas called water vapour

Index